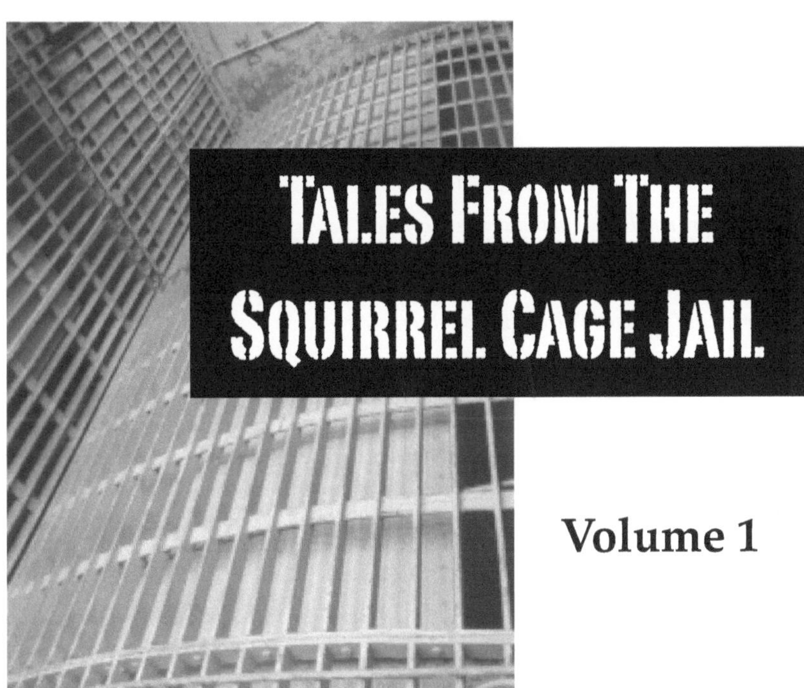

Volume 1

A collection of stories from the 84 years the unique rotary cell jail served Pottawattamie County.

"Kind of creepy, sometimes sad, and occasionally humorous. Sort of like the jail itself."

AF471795

Ryan Roenfeld
with Dr. Richard Warner
for
The Historical Society of Pottawattamie County, Iowa

Acknowledgments

The authors would like to thank the Historical Society of Pottawattamie, Gary and Barbara Roenfeld, Amanda Pokorski, Savannah Pokorski, Connor Hinshaw, John Paterson, Barbara Warner, and Steven Warner. Photographs courtesy of Ryan Roenfeld, Mike Warner, Barbara Warner, and Richard Warner unless otherwise noted.

About the Authors

Ryan Roenfeld is president of the Historical Society of Pottawattamie County and avid local history researcher and writer. In addition to his frequent articles in the Society's "Member Journal" Mr. Roenfeld has coauthored a number of books including "Council Bluffs: Broadway," "Omaha and Council Bluffs Yesterday and Today," "Council Bluffs: 365 Days, 150 Years," and "Council Bluffs Remembered."

Richard Warner has served as editor of the Historical Society of Pottawattamie County's "Member Journal" for over twenty years and is coauthor of the book "Council Bluffs: Broadway." Dr. Warner is a dentist in Council Bluffs and graduate of Creighton University (B.S. and D.D.S.) and the University of Nebraska at Omaha (M.A.).

Tales From the Squirrel Cage Jail was funded by the
Historical Society of Pottawattamie County,
Post Office Box 2, Council Bluffs, Iowa, 51502.
Copyright 2009

The Pottawattamie County "Squirrel Cage"

The unique "Squirrel Cage" in Council Bluffs served as the Pottawattamie County Jail from September 1885 until December 1969. This was America's largest rotary jail, an idea first patented in July 1881 by William Brown and Benjamin Haugh of Indianapolis. The purpose of the new facility was "to produce a jail in which prisoners can be controlled without the necessity of personal contact between them and the jailer." In addition, the rotary jail was designed to provide "maximum security with minimum jailer attention." In many ways, the rotary jail mirrored some of the theories behind Jeremy Bentham's Panopticon which was invented as "penal imprisonment, from the beginning of the nineteenth century, covered both the deprivation of liberty and the technical transformation of individuals."

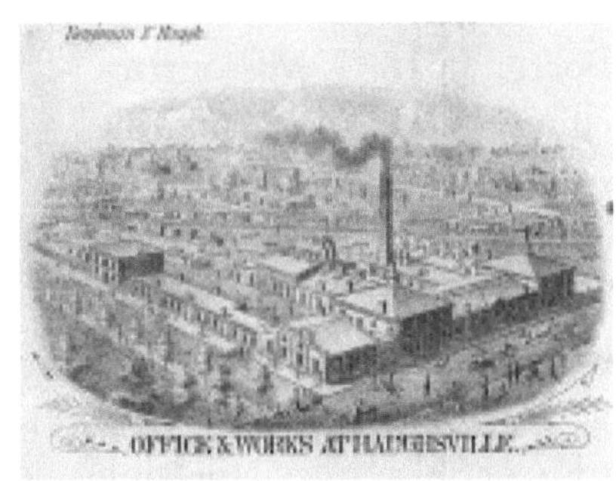

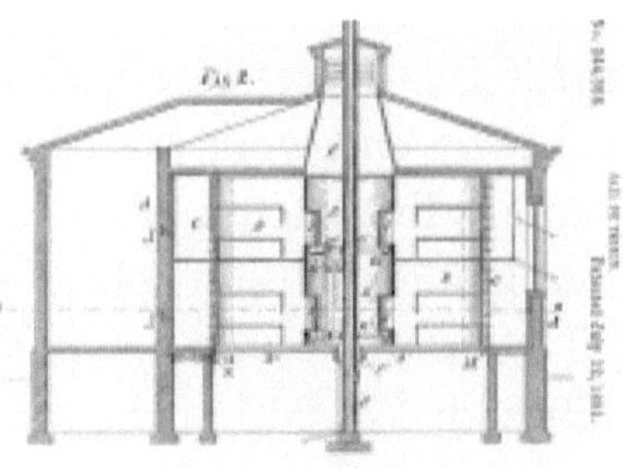

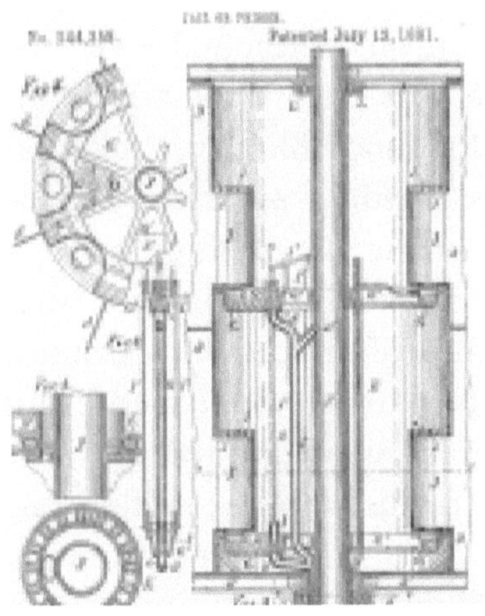

According to Michel Focault, the Panopticon consisted of cells arranged around a central tower, "so many cages, so many small theatres, in which each actor is alone, perfectly individualized and constantly visible." Strict segregation was intended for "individualizing observation, with characterization and classification, with the analytical arrangement of space."

Brown and Haugh's rotary jail dispensed with the central tower and constant observation in favor of a what one Iowa State Professor eventually called a "device in which human welfare had been sacrificed for security and the convenience of the jailer..."

In spite of future problems, the supposed effectiveness of the rotary jail and its low costs of operation soon came to the attention of the Pottawattamie County Board. In 1882, Missouri architects Eckel and Mann first supplied local officials with designs for a new county jail and members of the county board approved plans for the new jail two years later. In early 1885, county officials headed south to Missouri to inspect the jails at St. Joseph and Mayville. Finally, in what would become a rare occurrence through the years, a bond issue was passed in Pottawattamie County on March 10, 1885 with 5232 votes in favor of building a new courthouse and jail and 2933 opposed.

Missouri architects Eckel and Mann designed the building's exterior.

Bids to start construction of the new jail at 226 Pearl Street were opened in April 1885 and work was completed in just five months. According to the Council Bluffs Globe, the new jail cost the taxpayers not quite $30,000 with $21,000 of the sum for the metal from Haugh & Ketcham's Indiana foundry. General contractors were Wickham Brothers of Council Bluffs who also did all the masonry work. The outside walls of the jail are three layers of brick thick while all interior walls are two layers thick. Other Council Bluffs workers included John Epenter, who supplied the jail's metal cornice and slate roofing, carpenter G.S. Lawson, and painter B. Terwillinger.

The 28 foot tall cylinder rotated inside of a fixed metal cage (left). The 90,000 pound cylinder was suspended from an iron beam on the fourth floor (above).

Operation

The jail's rotary cylinder remained in operation for 75 years although it suffered from a variety of malfunctions from almost the beginning. The cylinder is 28 feet high, 24 feet in diameter, weighs just over 90,000 pounds empty, and is suspended from an iron beam on the fourth floor. The cylinder, cage, and all other metalwork was shipped to Council Bluffs from the Haugh and Ketcham Ironworks outside Indianapolis. The cylinder has

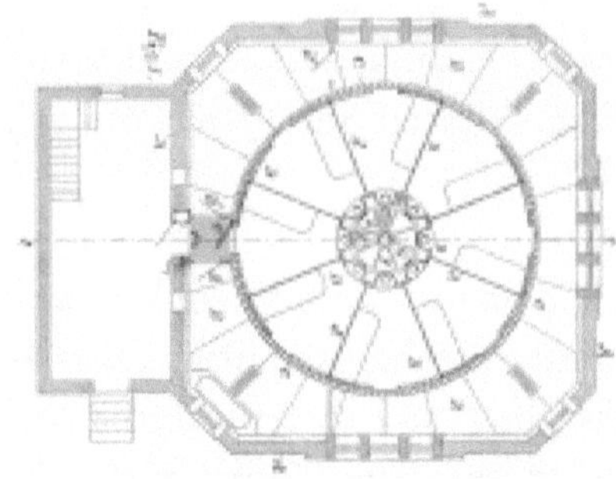

An individual pie-shaped cell (left) had to be lined up with the lone opening in the outer cage (see diagram at right from patent application) for a prisoner to get in or out of a cell.

three floors with ten pie shaped cells on each floor designed to hold two prisoners per cell. Since there was only one entrance or exit per floor the entire cylinder had to be turned with a hand-crank until the cell was lined up with the opening in the cage. For additional security, a water wheel was also reputedly used to continuously rotate the Squirrel Cage at night when the Jailer went to bed. Undoubtedly, the resulting racket would make sleep almost impossible and any evidence of this power source was removed long ago.

Theodore Guittar was the first sheriff at the "Squirrel Cage" jail.

The Early Years

The Sheriff of Pottawattamie County during construction of the Squirrel Cage was Theodore Guittar. Born in St. Louis, Theodore's father Francis came to the Council Bluffs during the late 1820's and worked for the American Fur Company at Traders Point on the Missouri River. The elder Guittar had gone independent by 1852 when he relocated his Indian trade-goods store a dozen or so miles north to a log cabin on West Broadway at the east side of Main Street. Guittar later ran a grocery a few blocks south where Theodore spent his early years working as a clerk until he joined the 2nd Iowa Light Artillery during the Civil War. He then came back to Council Bluffs, married his wife Elizabeth in 1869, and farmed east of town until he was appointed Deputy Sheriff in 1875. A Republican, Theodore Guittar was elected Constable of Council Bluffs in 1877 and was then elected Sheriff of Pottawattamie County in 1881 and again in 1883.

And on the afternoon of September 11, 1885 the Council Bluffs Globe reported that Sheriff Guittar, Jailer Schontz, and Constable McFadden had moved the first inmates into the jail. The first guests at the Squirrel Cage included murderer Cuff Johnson, horse-thief Miles Mullen, forger Frank Scofield, confidence man Ed Rankin, bootlegger John Gordon, and Mr. and Mrs. Brock who had been transferred from Manning, Iowa with their teenaged daughter and were all imprisoned under charges of larceny.

For the next 84 years the jail would host a colorful mix of prisoners although as early as 1887 the Globe declared the Squirrel Cage "pretty near a failure" as it would not rotate properly on its axis.

In March 1896, the Council Bluffs Nonpareil reported that the previous jailer had left the jail in a "filthy condition" for newly elected Sheriff Morgan. The jail, which held 32 prisoners at the time, was renovated and cleaned with three new coats of paint added inside. The cylinder itself was painted three different colors, the walls were painted white, and the stairs and railings jet black. The cost of the renovation was $1,000, which included a new supply of bedding for prisoners.

On a Monday night in early July 1896 someone robbed Jim Coyle's Saloon on South 21st Street between 8th and 9th Avenues. Pilfered items included whiskey, several boxes of cigars, and a slot machine containing $20 worth of nickels. The slot machine was discovered the next morning (emptied of its contents, of course) under a platform at the nearby Union Pacific rail yards. Council Bluffs resident Edward Kesler was accused of the crime and was arrested at his job at American Biscuit Manufacturing in Omaha. He was hauled across the river in front of Judge Vien and pled not guilty but was sent to the Squirrel Cage nonetheless as he could not come up with the money for bail.

A few weeks later a Pottawattamie County posse set out to scour the countryside after it was reported that Frank Ward and W.E. St. John were on their way back to Council Bluffs. Ward and St. John were both wanted for a string of robberies in Mapleton, River Sioux, Salix, and several other points on the Missouri between Council Bluffs and Sioux City. The posse discovered the accused thieves camped out north of town at Mynster Springs in the company of the "notorious" Kit Lawson along with four mules, a horse, and two wagons loaded with stolen merchandise. The men claimed to be horse-traders but the Nonpareil assured its readers that the "men travel from place to place making a living by stealing anything they can lay their hands on." The posse hauled Ward and St. John down to the Squirrel Cage in Council Bluffs while Ms. Lawson, notorious or not, was sent on her merry way.

In February 1903, Mrs. Barney McDaniels and Bert Levix were hauled to the Squirrel Cage after they were arrested in Macedonia for the murder of Mr. McDaniels. The duo were acquitted of the crime three months later but were advised not to return to Macedonia. Nine months later in November 1903 Ed Canning was elected to his first term as Pottawattamie County Sheriff. Born in Council Bluffs, Canning left school at the age of 17, trained as a machinist, and got married to his wife Lenora out in Denver in 1885. Canning was elected City Marshall of Council Bluffs in 1894 and served for four years. He then went back to working as a machinist at the Union Pacific shops in Council Bluffs until 1900 when he was appointed a Deputy Sheriff.

Although a Grand Jury had found the jail in "good, sanitary condition" in 1902, the Nonpareil reported in August 1904 that the Squirrel Cage got stuck for three days. The rotary cage was "used only at night" and during the day the ten prisoners then incarcerated were "let out into the corridor". Four years later in 1908, a different Grand Jury condemned the Squirrel Cage and dubbed it a "crusty clink" health hazard. The Jail would ultimately be condemned by numerous similar Grand Juries over the years, mostly for the same reasons, and typically send the Sheriff and county officials scrambling to find the necessary funds to keep the place operational.

Early Escapes From the "Squirrel Cage"

There were numerous escape attempts out of the jail, some of them violent, some humorous, and quite a few even successful. Where there's a will there always seems to be a way and at no time in the jail's history was the Squirrel Cage ever escape proof.

One of the first, and largest, escapes from the Squirrel Cage occurred in December 1888. The Council Bluffs Nonpareil called it "one of the boldest and most successful deliveries on record in the state" after eleven prisoners fled out the front door of the jail at four o'clock in the afternoon. The last man out, named Mulligan, was a bit too slow and was tackled right outside the front door by Matron O'Neil's nephew. Two more escapees, named Johnson and Diamond, were soon recaptured near the Union Park horse track at Avenue A and North 15th Street after a half-mile foot-chase. The duo had been sentenced the week before to four years in the state penitentiary after being found guilty of burglarizing Crippen's General Store in Neola. Another escapee, named Aull, was captured later that afternoon. The remaining escaped prisoners included Leonards, Wood, Shoemaker, Sullivan, Raymond, Reynolds, and Ferguson. The prisoners had apparently filed through a lock between the dining/exercise area and the main bullpen and then scaled the rotary cage to the third floor where there were no prisoners and nothing was locked. With undoubtedly no small amount of glee, the group then fled down the three flights of iron stairs and right out the front door. The newspaper accused county employees of the "grossest negligence" for failing to secure all locks and for not periodically examining the locks for evidence of tampering.

John T. Hazen was elected Sheriff in November 1890 with an annual salary of over $6,000. He was the only Democrat that managed to get elected in Pottawattamie County that year and was also somewhat unusual for residing well outside of Council Bluffs. Born in Dearborn County, Indiana, Hazen came to Iowa with his family as a child. Following the death of his first wife, Hazen headed west in 1871 and settled on an 80 acre farm six miles southeast of Avoca. Most of the county was still open prairie and his first home was a tent. Hazen eventually moved into Avoca and married his second wife. Until he got elected Sheriff, Hazen worked as an auctioneer and his ability to speak both High and Low German was considered a particular asset.

In early January 1892 Sheriff Hazen discovered the escape of six prisoners after the "regulation amount of boarders did not show up" for breakfast. The prisoners had rigged "an old clock spring" and the "blade of a pair of scissors" with handles and "niched up in saw fashion" to cut an 8 by 12 inch hole through the bars and wiggle their way out. The escaped prisoners were 24 year old Harvey Moore, 24 year old William Stewart, both "incarcerated on charge of intent to kill", E. Ward was in jail for larceny, 35 year old Jack O'Donnell and 28 year old William Douglass had robbed a man in Neola, and Ed Fegley was in jail for beating his wife. Fegley, incidentally, was re-captured the same day he escaped after a Pottawattamie Deputy discovered him hiding behind a newly constructed fake wall in his Council Bluffs home.

One of the most violent escapes out of the Squirrel Cage took place in June 1902 when seven of eleven prisoners picked a lock and confronted Jailer Martin and his wife as the two were finishing up supper in the kitchen. The prisoners beat Martin and locked both him and his wife up in a cell before fleeing out the front door. The seven escapees were Mike Fahey, 23, who was in jail for robbery; 20 year old Mike Sheehan, also in jail for robbery; John Obreicht, E.G. Jones, and William Mason were all incarcerated for breaking and entering; H.S. Fishburn was in for larceny; and Andrew Thompson was in the Squirrel Cage for burglary. Sheriff L.B. Cousins offered a $50 reward each for Fahey, Sheehan, Jones and Mason and a $25 reward apiece for the other three. An inspection tour of the jail by Sheriff Cousins and the County Board of Supervisors the next day led to several changes, including cutting peepholes in the three iron doors that led into the Squirrel Cage with mesh steel screens placed just inside. H.S. Fishburn was recaptured a few days later skulking around the Rock Island rail yards with a skeleton key that had been fashioned out of a pewter spoon.

Occasional escapes continued and in September 1919 George Williams, alias Edward Franklin, the "Negro trusty" at the Squirrel Cage, was half way through a thirty day sentence when he slipped away "without saying good-bye." A tip led police to Williams' Omaha home and he was brought back to the Squirrel Cage "where he probably will dispense with the open air until his time is out."

As the Squirrel Cage aged, escapes became increasingly common no matter how many modifications were made. The jail was 53 years old in 1938 when Dallas Birt escaped by forcing a hole through the ceiling of the third-floor infirmary. He then climbed out on the steep-pitched roof covered with slick slate shingles and slid down a ventilation pipe to freedom. But Birt was back in jail before long after his father turned him in. Four years later in 1942, Birt escaped out of the jail again, this time by sawing a bar out of a second-story window, wiggling his way out, and dropping to the ground below. According to the newspaper he was recaptured just four days later while in the possession of burglar's tools.

Dallas Birt escaped by forcing a hole through the ceiling of the third floor infirmary.

In November 1944 two small-time hoodlums named John Giles and Edgar Cook busted their way out of the Nebraska penitentiary at Lincoln. They didn't get far though and found themselves thrown in the Pottawattamie County Jail. The pair soon managed to get themselves a hack-saw blade and began to saw their way out of Squirrel Cage. However, their plot was discovered before fruition and they were taken across the street to the Council Bluffs City Jail. And in January 1945 Giles and Cook managed to escape through several locked steel doors and made their way down into the basement and then outside. And that's when they stole a city police car to complete their escape from Council Bluffs. Supposedly they made imprints of the locks with cigarette papers and then modified a toothbrush and wooden spoon into skeleton keys. Dubbed the "Toothbrush Twins" by the national press, Giles and Cook headed east across the country stealing cars and thieving. The law caught up with them in Concord, New Hampshire a few weeks later.

In July 1949 prisoners Leon Ross and Floyd Peterson walked away from the jail unnoticed during church services conducted by the Salvation Army. Ross was serving six months for breaking and entering after he was convicted of burglarizing a café in Crescent and had just 23 days left of his sentence to serve. No stranger to authorities, according to the newspaper Ross had been in trouble since he was 14, had been kicked out of the Iowa Boys Home in Eldora for inciting a riot and smacking the warden, and had earned the nickname "The Jackrabbit" for his numerous escapes from juvenile authorities. Peterson had been incarcerated for bigamy and had already served two months of his six month sentence. Both prisoners were quickly recaptured, Peterson in Anaconda, Montana and Ross on the west coast.

Five prisoners escaped through a hole just a foot square on the jail's 64th birthday in 1949.

Just two months later, Peterson and Ross escaped out of the jail again on September 11, 1949, the Squirrel Cage's 64th birthday. The World-Herald reported that Peterson, Ross, Raymond Deputy, Hutchie Hutchison, and Missourian Charles Peine had all escaped through a hole cut through the iron wall of the bullpen that was just a foot square in size. Eight prisoners remained behind in the jail. Deputy was serving time for Grand Larceny and Peine and Hutchison were at the Squirrel Cage for stealing a car in Council Bluffs and then getting caught with it in Memphis, Tennessee.

Lynch Mobs

Overall, the Squirrel Cage had far less success in holding prisoners inside than with keeping lynch mobs out. That security feature was probably intentional as several such hangings had taken place previously in Council Bluffs. And while no lynch mob was ever successful, there were several close calls. One of the first took place in 1894 after crooked foot-racer and gambler Leon Lozier was accused of molesting a five year old neighbor girl at a duplex at 1115 Avenue D. By nightfall, a restless mob estimated at 2,000 people had gathered out in front of the Jail where Sheriff Hazen, four deputies, Council Bluffs Chief of Police John Scanlan, and three city police officers stood blocking the front door. A black man named John Berger reputedly forced his way to the front of the crowd and shouted that if the Lozier would have been black they would have already lynched him. "Give me the rope, I will lead the crowd!" Berger cried out before officers escorted him from the premises. To help control the situation, 29 militiamen armed with Winchester Rifles were called out from the nearby Dodge Light Guards Armory. The frustrated lynch mob slowly dispersed after midnight and Lozier was taken to the Mills County Jail in Glenwood for safekeeping.

Something similar took place on July 5th, 1895 after George Immerine was arrested for assaulting a 13 year old girl. The town was abuzz with rumors that a lynch mob was planning on storming the Squirrel Cage to hold a neck-tie party with Immerine the guest of honor. The talk grew prevalent enough for Sheriff Pryor to request the help of the Dodge Light Guards, but in the end the talk proved to be just talk.

In December 1903, a month after Ed Canning was elected Sheriff, several Council Bluffs women reported being robbed of their belongings while walking down the street. Police were eventually led to a four bedroom "shack" at 1508 3rd Avenue where several stolen items were recovered and two black men, Neely Zimmerman and George Burk, were arrested. The pair were taken to the Squirrel Cage and placed in the top tier of cells and rotated away from the platform. At the same time, the keys to all cells were taken out of the jail as five deputies, with orders to "shoot to kill," put up steel barricades and armed themselves with Winchesters, re-

To avert a possible jail break the two suspects were put in the top tier of cells and rotated away from the platform. Keys to all cells were taken out of the jail and five jailers ordered to "shoot to kill."

peating shotguns, and revolvers. Their fears proved well founded as a lynch mob gathered out front with ex-convict "Dutch" Stevenson and a few others urging the crowd to storm the jail. The militia was called out at a quarter to one in the morning to help restore order and were backed up by 50 local citizens determined to avert any hanging. The crowd slowly faded away although the soldiers remained in position in front of the jail until 4:30 the next morning. "Dutch" Stevenson was arrested the next day for attempting to incite a riot. It soon came out that his real motive was to use the confusion to free his criminal associate W.C. Rogers who was incarcerated in the jail charged with killing Bert Forney while robbing Forney's saloon at 1028 West Broadway. Nonetheless, Sheriff's deputies spirited Zimmerman and Burk out of town later that day for safekeeping before trial.

Infant Locked up in "Squirrel Cage"

Juveniles, sometimes even infants, were also locked up at the Squirrel Cage and the results of an armed standoff in November 1901 was just one of many occasions. The incident arose after a District Court Judge ordered the forced eviction of Emma Edwards and her six children from the farm where they had peacefully lived the past seven years. The property in question was situated six miles northwest of Crescent on accreted Missouri River bottom land legally claimed by W.H. Woods of Missouri Valley without regard for the people who had "squatted" there after the river moved. No doubt the proximity of the new Illinois Central railroad station at Ascot played a part in sudden outside interest in bottom lands previously left to mosquitoes, muskrats, and a plucky few like Mrs. Edwards who was described in the newspaper as "a little woman and has an infant not a year old, but was quite handy with a big revolver.." Emma also found strong support from several neighbors loathe to let some Judge down in Council Bluffs force the family into homelessness as blood, sweat, and tears constituted legal title far more than any fancy document.

Mrs. Edwards was declared in contempt of court after she chased off county agents at gunpoint. Armed deputies were soon sent and busted into her home as she fired over their heads insisting that she and her family would remain on their land or "someone would get shot." Eventually subdued, Mrs. Edwards was hauled down to the Squirrel Cage with her youngest child and two neighbors, Charles and Jerry Belt. More arrests soon followed, including Fred Ruby, Roderick Vincent, and Emma's oldest child, 16 year old Kirk Edwards. After two days sitting in the Squirrel Cage with her baby, Mrs. Edwards bonded out for $300. However, instead of leaving Kirk behind, she returned with her infant the next day to take his place and sent him to look after the rest of the children. There was "blood on the moon" at Crescent over the encounter and nine belligerents were eventually hauled to the county jail before it was over. After an additional two days in the Squirrel Cage, friends raised another $300 to bail Emma Edwards and her infant out for the second time and only three of her nine sympathetic neighbors charged in the affair still remained behind bars.

Mrs. Edwards was described as "a little woman and has an infant not a year old, but was quite handy with a big revolver."

Francisco Guidice and the Council Bluffs Race Riot of 1913

Probably the worst attempted lynching at the Squirrel Cage took place on the evening of May 2, 1913 after Howard Jones was murdered near the Chicago & Northwestern railroad roundhouse at 1100 Avenue A. The failed lynching quickly erupted into the most violent race riot in the history of Council Bluffs. The intended victim of the lynch mob was Francisco Guidice, aka Henry Wiley, an Italian immigrant laborer recently fired from the railroad. It quickly became apparent that Guidice would not be safe at the Squirrel Cage, or anywhere else in Council Bluffs, and he was secreted away to the Harrison County Jail in Logan where he confessed to the murder in a hand-written statement.

"Mob Ravages Italian Quarters" trumpeted the headline in the Nonpareil the day after the failed lynching and Judge Wheeler ordered special session of the Grand Jury to convene on Saturday morning to investigate. The newspaper reported that "Groups of shivering Italians and Greeks clustered about the railroad yards of the city, undecided whether to return to work or leave the city, and shattered fronts in practically all of the Greek and Italian business houses on central Broadway, were the only reminders..."

The Nonpareil reported that at 10:30 on Thursday night a mob estimated at 150 "led by residents of South Omaha and Boone, Iowa" demanded that Jailer Heller turn over the accused murderer. The World-Herald estimated the crowd at the Squirrel Cage at "several thousand" who had gathered at Cochran Park on 1st Avenue and marched en masse downtown. According to the Omaha newspaper, Jailer Heller actually allowed seven men

The murder of Howard Jones at the Chicago & Northwestern roundhouse touched off the most violent race riot in Council Bluffs history.

from the mob inside the Squirrel Cage just to prove that Guidice wasn't even there. The "howling mob with no leaders" were not satisfied and chanted "Kill the Dagoes" as the failed lynching turned its fury on the neighborhood. The mobs first target was John Birbilis' Palace of Sweets at 4 Pearl Street. Windows were smashed and the interior quickly wrecked causing at least $300 in damages. Next to fall victim was the O.K. Lunch Room at 529 West Broadway which was said to be run by William Sitheris. Windows and dishes were also smashed at the lunch room operated by Frank Antone at 535 West Broadway. Across the street from Antone's was a restaurant and pool hall also operated and frequented by Greeks. The immigrant patrons fled the building while the American cook stood his ground to face down the mob, later telling the newspaper that it was a "bad night for the Greeks." Ultimately, three candy stores, three lunch rooms, a barbershop, and one shoe shine parlor, all run by Greeks, were ravaged by the mob. Around 200 or so rioters then made their way up North 8th Street to the Italian neighborhood near the Northwestern roundhouse where homes were ransacked, several people were hauled out into the streets and beaten, and just one man was arrested for the incident. According to the World-Herald, "Italians in Omaha ready to send over rifles" to Council Bluffs where city officials were preparing to declare martial law.

"Declare war on All Foreigners" read the next day's headline which described the mobs goal of "running every Italian and Greek out of the city." The Nonpareil reported receiving a telephone call from one of the purported ringleaders who said he was a Northwestern employee who lived on 1st Avenue. The man said that there would be a mass meeting that night at 14th and West Broadway intending on "visiting every Italian, Greek, Austrian, Japanese, and Chinese person in the city" who would be given 48 hours to leave Council Bluffs for good. The caller estimated the previous night's mob at 350 and promised a crowd of at least 750 that night with local resi-

Cochran Park on First Avenue where a crowd estimated at several thousand gathered to march en masse to the "Squirrel Cage" jail.

General Matt Tinley in 1940.

dents joined by like-minded compatriots who were headed to Council Bluffs from Missouri Valley and Boone.

Needless to say, Council Bluffs Mayor Thomas Maloney was justifiably "Indignant" over the affair and claimed that "I don't look for any trouble tonight but if trouble comes we will be prepared." Maloney disputed participation by locals and promised that "Our city will not be overrun again by a bunch of Nebraska hoodlums." To forestall violence, the Dodge Light Guards were out in force, all police reserves were on duty, and it was "probable that a number of deputy sheriffs sworn in." Major Matt Tinley of the Iowa National Guard was also prepared to bring three additional companies of militia from nearby towns into Council Bluffs where the World-Herald warned that "Police will fire on rioters..." The Northwestern Railroad was cooperating with police and Mayor Maloney pronounced that "Last night's affair was a disgrace. Not one of the Greeks whose property was damaged was in any way connected with the murder of Jones..."

Not surprisingly, Judge Wheeler moved Guidice's trial down to Glenwood at the request of the accused with the Mills County Tribune noting the "Aroused state of public feeling" in Council Bluffs. Prosecutors wanted Guidice to hang for the crime and the Pottawattamie County Sheriff was required to deliver the accused to Sheriff Bushnell to be held without bail at the Mills County Jail. The Tribune also reported that additional deputies would be required since "Several of the Italians in the Pottawattamie county jail, as accessories to the crime of murder after the fact, will be brought to Glenwood as witnesses...."

The murder trial was reported in detail by the Tribune, including the testimony of J.G. Fogle, machinist at the Northwestern roundhouse, on the origins of the dispute. According to Fogle, the ill-will between Guidice and Jones began after "the Italian" refused to put a head light reflector on Jones' locomotive. When Harrison County Sheriff O.O. Rock was called to the stand Guidice's hand-written confession was introduced as Exhibit 8. The newspaper also reported the testimony of Mrs. Frances Coffman of 1029 Avenue D who had been with Guidice at the Majestic Theater on the night of the murder. According to Mrs. Coffman, Guidice had told her on two different occasions that he would "get even with Jones and would leave a scar on him for life." Coffman claimed to have talked him out of it while the newspaper made insinuations over a married woman with one child being familiar enough with the accused to call him "Henry".

Samuel Mancusco of Omaha was called on to serve as interpreter for the Italians incarcerated at the Squirrel Cage as accessories, including William Porche, a cinder pit worker at the Northwestern roundhouse who roomed in the same house as Guidice. The Tribune reported that "strong statements for the state were secured" from Porche who identified the blood-stained razor, Exhibit 9, as being owned by the accused. Porche also testified that he found Guidice in his bed the night of the murder and told him that "Jones is dead and he wrote your name" and that Guidice then dressed and rushed out of the house, leaving behind the razor "covered with blood, upon the bed."

Eight men and one woman were called to testify the next day, including Mrs. Josephine Foraggi, the housekeeper at Guidice's boarding house, who was on the stand for two hours and fifteen minutes talking through the interpreter. Dominick Sesto, an Italian who lived in the home where Guidice was arrested, testified that the accused showed up at his house at 12:20 at night and explained that he was locked out of his room and that if police happened to show up to tell them that he had arrived at 9:30. According to Sesto, Guidice also told him to tell Tony O'Roberts to hide his razor and gun if he was arrested.

Fred Miley, a Northwestern fireman who lived at 218 Stutsman, told the court that he had run into Guidice the afternoon of the murder at 11th and West Broadway. Miley testified that Guidice had asked him when Jones was due back at the roundhouse and then went into a saloon on the corner. T. F. Callaghan, Chief Detective of the Council Bluffs Police department, also took the stand and testified that Guidice was arrested at 1307 Avenue D by himself, Detective Lane, and two railroad special agents. He said the accused was in bed and offered no resistance. The court also heard from Engineer Skaith who had been with Jones the night he was murdered and from Mr. Barnet who testified that the accused had told him that he would get even with Jones for getting him fired.

After a long day in court the Italians held as accessories, Mr. and Mrs. Frank Foraggi, Dominick Sesto, William Porche, and Mike Longo were all hauled back up to the Squirrel Cage in Council Bluffs until they were needed again. According to the Tribune, "Large crowds are in attendance all the time and the women appear to be especially interested in this case." Guidice was described as "holding his own well" and that he arrived in court every morning in a "clean shirt, a press in his trousers and a clean shaven face."

The Nonpareil reported on July 2nd that Northwestern employee John Wakehouse and Jack Bowen, "accused of having been the leader of the mob" that rampaged across downtown, had both been charged with "inciting the unlawful killing of a human being". The next day on July 3rd, the Tribune reported that Guidice had been found guilty of first degree murder and sentenced to life at hard labor at penitentiary in Ft. Madison. The jury had deliberated for two hours before announcing their decision. Defense Attorney Hess' request for a new trial based on the "usual stereotyped reasons, together with allegations of misconduct of counsel…" was denied by Judge Arthur. Guidice cried when his fate was announced and smiled at the jury. The newspaper reported that he "said in broken English that 'they did not hang me,'" but claimed he was innocent of the murder of Howard Jones to the end.

The five Italians held in jail as accessories were also set free on July 3rd to spend an undoubtedly interesting Independence Day. A week later Jack Bowen pled guilty to lesser charges for his involvement in the riots and was sentenced to 90 days sitting in the Squirrel Cage. Thanks to the vigilance of historian Beverly Boileau of Glenwood, Iowa, Guidice's hand written confession and the straight razor used to kill Howard Jones are now on permanent display at the Squirrel Cage Jail.

Immorality, Bootlegging, and The King of the Gypsies

In early 1918, Iowa State Agent Rock claimed that Council Bluffs had been swept by an "epidemic of immorality" and set out to sweep vice from the city. Maude Ables and Bessie Greco were hauled down to the Squirrel Cage in July 1918 after they were arrested at Manawa and charged with prostitution while a large number of others were sent to the Creche, a home for the wayward. In all, ten women were eventually sentenced. Those swept up in the crusade against vice included 15 year old Frances Wright, 16 year old Lorena Anderson, 16 year old Marie Cairns, 18 year old Christina Dettman, and 16 year old Lucile Harden, who were all found guilty of lewdness; 15 year old Eleanor Dettman was found guilty of delinquency; and 19 year old Carrie Bell Allen was found guilty of prostitution. Most of the women were paroled into the custody of others while Lucile Harden and Eleanor Dettman were sent to Mitchellville until they turned 21 and Christina Dettman was sentenced to six months in Rockwell City. Maude Ables was sentenced to five years at Rockwell City but the Judge agreed to let her go as long as she left Council Bluffs. The fate of Bessie Greco remains unknown.

The Creche at 807 Pierce Street in Council bluffs was established in 1906 as a refuge for homeless children.

Horse thief J.M. Lee was apprehended by Deputy Sheriff Gillaspy in August 1918 after a two mile chase through "backyards, buildings, and alleys" around downtown Council Bluffs that finally ended with Lee surrendering while standing on the stage of the Danish Hall at Glen Avenue and West Broadway. Reportedly, a suspicious woman had called Sheriff Bill Groneweg after Lee had tried to sell her a team of horses far too cheaply. One of Gillaspy's bullets grazed Lee during the chase and he begged the Deputy not to shoot him dead on stage. Instead, Gillaspy hauled him down to the Squirrel Cage where Lee quickly confessed to stealing the team of horses out of the Goehning pasture near Carson.

In September 1918, Jailer Kinsell and Sheriff Groneweg discovered one bar missing from the rotary and another loose enough to allow someone to slip into bullpen. They also found tampering with the windows. Kinsell and Groneweg then staked out the Jail for the next three nights and patiently observed prisoners Louis Dolson and George McClendan "diligently" sawing through the bars on one of the west windows of the bullpen. Jess Howard's cell faced the "scene of sawing operations" and Jailer Kinsell believed that Howard was the "chief engineer" of the attempted break-out. Kinsell also discovered several broken saws inside Howard's cell, along with evidence of outside help as someone had slipped the saws through the windows. However, the prisoners apparently grew too nervous to continue their plans as the night work suddenly ceased. They were transferred into new cells soon after while workers repaired the damage. The next week Howard and McClendan both pled guilty to automobile theft and were sentenced five years each in Ft. Madison.

In spite of its justifiably notorious reputation, a few good times at the jail also made their way into the newspaper. One November 1918 article described the annual Thanksgiving dinner given to the 30 men and one woman then incarcerated at the Squirrel Cage where the "hospitality of the jailer and the home cooking of his wife, brought smiles to the faces of each unfortunate and they were the recipients of hearty and sincere congratulations." The Thanksgiving dinner served to prisoners that year included celery soup, a Prohibition-era Manhattan cocktail, the "Kaiser's Goat" (which was reportedly intentionally too tough to eat), roast goose with dressing, mashed potatoes, creamed peas, olives, bread and butter, coffee, assorted pies a la mode, and cigarettes.

The failed prohibition of alcoholic beverages during the early 20th century probably brought more people down to the Squirrel Cage than anything else in its history. A sampling of bootleggers from 1918 included one-time Deputy Sheriff Peter J Juel, alias J. Brown, and his accomplice Carl Cook, alias Jim Peterson, who were arrested in May by Federal agent Sumner Knox. In September, Omahans William and Albert Fox, John Van Meter, and G.D. Huston were arrested during a raid at the J.H. Garner farm five miles north of Council Bluffs while they were busy loading 325 pints of alcohol stored in caskets into a hearse. That Halloween, Judge Wade incarcerated Sam McCormack, the black porter at a West Broadway barbershop, for bootlegging. McCormack had already spent four months in jail awaiting trial and Judge Wade pronounced "Well, I'll give you six months more and see if that will cure you. If not, come back again..." Albert Lattery had been at the jail for four months on the same charge and was sentenced to an additional eight months in the county jail. That same day, 17 year old Ralph Barker was sentenced to 40 days in the jail for a liquor violation. The next week, a blind man named John Lehr was sentenced to six months in the Squirrel Cage for bootlegging.

Then in November 1919, the Squirrel Cage was involved in a dispute between two gypsy tribes over two teenaged girls. According to newspaper clippings, Frank Mitchell of Philadelphia, the "King of All Gypsies", came to Council Bluffs claiming that his daughter Rosie and a girl named Sophie Karmenovitch Guannalch had been abducted. Mitchell was accompanied by Sophie's brother Joe Guannalch and they had tracked the two missing girls to a group of gypsies camped out in Council Bluffs at 828 Avenue I. The pleas of Mitchell and Guannalch convinced the Council Bluffs police to raid the encampment headed by Mullis "Steve" Marks where the two girls were quickly recovered. During the raid, Mitchell was nearly killed by an irate Annie Marks who "tried to carve him with a butcher knife." Twenty-five gypsies soon found themselves at the Council Bluffs police station with some claiming that the girls had been "bought" under a "binding legal system which is perfectly legal" while Mitchell and Guannalch insisted that the two girls had been kidnapped from their camp the previous March. It was decided to let Judge Capell sort it out in the morning and Mitchell, Guannalch, and the two girls were sent to the Neumayer Hotel on West Broadway.

In the meantime, the Marks band got busy and returned at midnight with a warrant issued in Hobbard, Ohio for the arrest of Mitchell for grand larceny. It soon came out that the Marks bunch had paid $2,600 for the two girls and then had a "John Doe" warrant issued, just in case someone tried to get them back. The two girls in question, one 12 and the other 14, were reportedly "well developed for their age, tall thin, brown skinned girls, very pretty in their oriental colors and their Arabian costumes which are covered with embroidered roses and flowers in their natural hues." The girls refused to be photographed unless they were paid first and the newspaper reported that the gypsy leaders sported "rolls of bills that would 'choke several cows,' not in ones either, but in twenties and fifties..." made from telling fortunes and horse trading. The case quickly "took on a new angle" after Federal Inspector Daily in Omaha ordered Marks and the two girls held at the Squirrel Cage for investigation by federal authorities into possible violations of the Mann Act. At the same time, Associated Press coverage of the fray led to the arrest of Frank Mitchell and gypsy Joe Evans at the request of

Sheriff Groneweg complained to federal officials that the gypsies were "harder to get rid of than a bum dollar..."

law enforcement in Superior and Duluth, Minnesota on suspicion of involvement in a "big diamond robbery" along with several other thefts while they had been in Council Bluffs. Also thrown in the Squirrel Cage was Amelia Marks, held on a charge of theft of a diamond ring in Omaha, and another gypsy who was suspected of stealing five cigar boxes out of Beaton's Drug store in Omaha.

And then, according to the headline, "The city, state, and federal authorities dismiss action against the tribes" as the "rumpus between rival gypsy clans" came to an abrupt end and all prisoners were released on a Friday morning. Apparently, the gypsies had "simply camped in the corridor of the courthouse from the time it was opened until the closing hour at night" for three days straight and the local clans had been joined by a delegation from Dubuque and another from Duluth, Minnesota. "Why should we not come when our friends are in trouble?" one of them asked the reporter. At the same time, Sheriff Groneweg appealed to federal officials that the gypsies were "harder to get rid of than a bum dollar..." In the end, the U.S. Attorney General recommended that local officials forget about the whole thing and let the gypsies settle it for themselves, which is what they had pretty much wanted in the first place.

That same month Kenneth Olson was fined $100 and sentenced to 60 days in the Squirrel Cage. Olson came from New England and was arrested after breaking into the farm of A.R. Fiori in Garner Township. He claimed that he "needed some clothing, having sold his extra clothing because he was short of money" when a "sudden cold snap caught him..." Jailer Orlie Kinsell probably had a similar cold snap the next month in December 1919 after he petitioned the Pottawattamie County Board for a raise. He requested a salary of $10 a month during the six months of the year that he was required to take care of the Jail's behemoth of a furnace with its hissing array of pipes and steam radiators. The county turned him down.

The gypsies camped in the corridor of the courthouse from the time it opened until closing.

Jake Bird

Perhaps the most infamous prisoner to spend time in the Squirrel Cage was Jake Bird who was either one of the worst serial killers of the early 20th century or merely a patsy willing to confess to anything to forestall his date of execution. Either way, Bird achieved nationwide notoriety in the late 1940's as the Tacoma Axe Murderer and an entire chapter was devoted to his exploits in John McCallum's 1978 book Crime Doctor which profiled the career of Dr. Charles Larson, the "world's foremost medical detective."

Born in Louisiana in 1901, Bird's profession as an iterant gandydancer who worked on the railroad lines undoubtedly attracted him to the area. Bird first came to the attention of local authorities in late 1928 after Mrs. Harold Stribling of Carter Lake identified him as the "axman who hacked herself and her husband in their home a week ago..." The attack happened as the couple slept with Mr. Stribling receiving several axe blows to the face before his wife woke up. The December 3, 1928 issue of Time magazine reported that Jake Bird "chopped at Mrs. Stribling, gashed her over the eye. She begged for mercy. 'Well, then, go and wash your face,' he said. He went with her, washed his hands. He asked to see her baby and stood over its crib for several minutes. Like a mother partridge playing broken-wing, she begged him to leave the house with her. He took her to the swamps on the edge of town. . . . She got to a hospital, half-crazed."

While laying in an Omaha hospital bed Mrs. Stribling told the newspapers that "I know absolutely that Bird is the man. I was with him too long to forget him." Originally held in Omaha, Bird's lawyer A.V. Shotwell said he would not fight extradition to Iowa and Bird was subjected to intense questioning by Pottawattamie County Sheriff Percy Lainson and County Attorney Frank Northrop. The interrogation lasted from 6 PM Monday night until 2 AM Tuesday morning but the newspaper reported that "Bird looked as unmoved and cool as he had been under the questioning of others for the last three days" and stuck to his alibi, reportedly saying "Give me a cigar" after his grilling by Sheriff Lainson. On December 8, Bird remained confident that his friends in Omaha would raise enough money to hire a good lawyer. According to the newspaper, "He sits for minutes staring fixedly ahead of him and often breaks into a profuse sweat while still in thought." At the same time, authorities were also pursuing

Bird's whereabouts at the time of the murder of Mrs. Walter Resso and her sister Creta Brown. Both women had been murdered the same night as the attack on the Striblings when Bird was reportedly at "Plantation Gardens, a Negro roadhouse within 2/3 of mile of the Resso home."

Bird was hauled over to the Squirrel Cage awaiting trial for the attack on the Striblings. According to jailhouse folklore, he spent his nights in the Pottawattamie County Jail screaming "Blood! Blood! Buckets of Blood!" over and over all night long. He was found guilty and sentenced to the state penitentiary at Ft. Madison. Harold Stribling, who had survived Bird's axe attack, was at the trial and Bird assured him that "I'll get you wherever you go."

Bird was released after 12 years in Ft. Madison and quickly left Iowa behind. Old habits died hard though as Jake Bird continued his murder spree across the country until October 1947 when he was apprehended in Tacoma, Washington. He was caught in an alley with his shoes in his hands and brains splattered across his pants behind a house where two murdered women lay inside. A one page confession was recorded a few hours after his arrest but Bird claimed that burglary was the motive and things just got out of hand. Dr. Larson, on the other hand, believed that Bird "got a gut-kick from seeing women with expressions of horror and fear on their faces" although he was "sharp as a tack, an avid reader, an able conversationalist and witty."

Convicted for murdering the two Tacoma women, Bird was sentenced to death in December 1947 and reputedly cursed the courtroom with the "Jake Bird hex" promising those present that "you will die before I do." Already suspected in several slayings across the country, as Bird's date of execution approached he confessed his involvement in up to 44 murders, with an axe his favored weapon. "My conscience don't hurt me…I ain't got no conscience," Jake Bird is quoted as saying by Dr. Larson although Bird assured him that "I wouldn't go so far as to say I killed somebody every night." Among Bird's admitted crimes were the robbing and killing an elderly woman in Pueblo, Colorado in 1942, stabbing an old man to death in bed in Ogden, Utah, and beating a small boy to death in South Bend, Indiana. Of all his victims, the murder of a boy in Carter Lake was the only one that he showed much remorse for. In fact, according to Bird, another convict confessed to that particular crime while Bird skulked around outside the courthouse during the trial.

Five people, including Bird's court-appointed lawyer and the judge, had died by the time Jake Bird finally met his end at the end of a rope in Walla Walla in 1949 after a last meal of fried chicken, bananas, strawberries, ice cream and orange pop. Among the witnesses to his execution was Harold Stribling who still had a metal plate in his head and had lived in fear that Bird would find him for the past 22 years. Although raised Catholic, Bird's last statement was read by a Lutheran minister: "The Lord giveth, the Lord taketh away. Blessed is the name of the Lord." Jake Bird hung for 14 minutes before he was pronounced dead.

The Dirty Thirties and a Farmer's Holiday

Jake Bird's sentence over the attack on the Striblings was just one of the 155 convictions handed down by the Pottawattamie County District Court in Council Bluffs during the fiscal year of 1928-29 and his wasn't even the worst. That dubious honor belonged to Clarence Lukehart who was sentenced to life in Ft. Madison after he pled guilty to the second degree murder of Harvey Boyd in East Omaha, as Carter Lake was still known. This was the murder that Jake Bird later expresed remorse for. The largest fine handed out by Pottawattamie County had been $1000 against Marvin Mercer. Convicted of possessing illegal narcotics, Mercer fled Council Bluffs only to be captured out on the west coast. Unable to pay the fine, Mercer was spending most of 1929 in the Squirrel Cage as part of his 10 month sentence. Pottawattamie County had spent $11,460.99 on "board for prisoners" between May 1928 and '29. That was a decrease of $46.74 from the previous fiscal year and Sheriff Percy Lainson assured taxpayers that "every cent" had been spent on the repair and upkeep of the county jails at Council Bluffs and Avoca. First elected Pottawattamie County Sheriff in 1922,

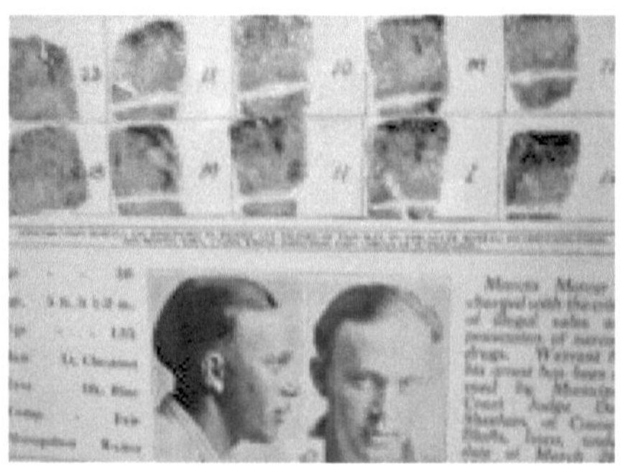

Wanted poster for Marvin Mercer on display at the Squirrel Cage jail.

"Perce" Lainson was a World War I hero who had joined the 168th Infantry at the age of 16. As Sheriff, Lainson brought a quick end to the box-car robberies that plagued the Council Bluffs rail yards and established the Pottawattamie County Vigilantes Association. Sheriff Lainson's Vigilantes included 18 patrols and 96 "heavily armed" men capable of blocking every major highway in the county with iron spikes in under six minutes. He also organized a regular Sheriffs patrol that would "cover all the entire county and that will visit every town on Wednesday and Saturday nights..." and was "ready to give all the help needed in the war on bootleggers and law breakers of every sort or kind." The World-Herald once called him "A stormy figure who could roar like a bull when angry with reporters on some issues but not a man to hold a grudge" whose "characteristic position" was "feet on a table, Stetson hat cocked over one eyebrow and a Bull Durham cigarette in his fingers..." The Carson Critic once boasted that Sheriff Lainson would go after a "bootlegger, a still or an auto gang, with the same smile he goes up against a pie counter or a midnight lunch."

Other prisoners over the summer of 1929 included Omahans William Burns and his wife who were given thirty days each in the Squirrel Cage for "disorderliness" by Judge Blanchard. Burns claimed the altercation was truly a case of mistaken identity and that it was really his brother who "was

said to have been too attentive" to a certain Mrs. George Budatz. However, when Officers Pat Bangs and C.E. McDaniels showed up at the Sunday night dispute the Burns couple were fighting Mr. Budatz on the sidewalk in front of his home at 610 West Washington Avenue. It was reported that Mrs. Burns had "tore the screen door off the house and broken a window" during the altercation although at her trial she testified that she was "just protecting" her husband who had really been mistaken for his brother. Mysteriously, the newspaper failed to note that the brother never showed up in court to defend his sibling. The officers, however, were quite willing to testify that the Burns couple used "abusive" language and were "cursing everyone present" when they were taken up to the Council Bluffs police station and city jail at Bryant and Vine Streets. In fact, Mrs. Burns had actually been taken out of the city jail three times that first night after complaints from neighbors about the wild ruckus.

On July 16th, 1929 47 year old J.L. Harbor of Colome, South Dakota pled guilty to forgery and Judge Dewell sentenced him to three months in the county jail. The charge against Harbor had been brought by August Sierck concerning a forged $200 check. The Nonpareil reminded readers that several years earlier both Sierck and Harbor had been charged with manslaughter over the shooting of one of their neighbors on the road between Treynor and Carson. Sierck had been acquitted on that charge while Harbor spent several years in the Iowa penitentiary.

Council Bluffs City Hall and Police Station at Bryant and Vine Streets.

Also on the 16th, Attorney Donald Rothrock applied for a pardon on behalf of Mrs Ada Poore Diggley of 1120 3rd Avenue. Mrs. Diggley had been sentenced to six months in the Squirrel Cage for contempt of court and violating the liquor laws. Her attorney claimed that there was insufficient evidence to convict her, she hadn't gotten a trial in front of a jury, and she was the mother of two young children. Oddly enough, Rothrock was brought up on charges of violating the liquor laws a month later but skipped town rather than face paying $1000 or sitting in the Squirrel Cage waiting on the Grand Jury.

And on July 20th Vincent Francis walked out the front doors of the Squirrel Cage a free man after spending a month behind bars for not paying alimony. His complaint during sentencing had been that he couldn't support both his previous and current wife on his salary of $110 a month from the Northwestern railroad. Francis was freed after coming to a new agreement with his old wife to forget about what he still owed and just pay her $10 a month.

The box-car robberies and bootlegging of the roaring 1920's seemed almost quaint as times grew grim and the Squirrel Cage sometimes exceeded its capacity of 85 prisoners. The worsening economic depression, drought, and the dustbowl out west made the '30's a dirty decade indeed. Many of the unemployed and homeless who crossed the country by rail found themselves in Council Bluffs where the Bonus Army camped out on their way to Washington to plead for relief. Nonetheless, until Iowa's prohibition laws were repealed in 1933 those who indulged in intoxicating spirits seemed to always have a home at the Squirrel Cage. That included Arthur Madison who was hauled down to the county jail with a small quantity of liquor in August of 1932. Madison was arrested after a raid by federal agents and Sheriff's deputies following a raid at his "ice and pop stand" at 23rd and West Broadway that officials suspected was operating as a "spiked beer joint".

An eight inch downpour had flooded the streets of Council Bluffs early that August and a crowd of over 300 people gathered a half-block north of the Squirrel Cage at Bayliss Park to listen to "General" Jacob Coxey give a speech. An old-time populist, Coxey was an Ohio quarry operator who had organized the 1894 march of the Industrial Army on Washington.

During his career Coxey had run for office, usually unsuccessfully, variously representing the Greenback, Populist, Republican, Democrat, and Union parties and had finally been elected Mayor of Massillion, Ohio, as a Republican, in 1931. But during that summer of 1932 the 78 year old Coxey was out on the road as the presidential candidate for the Farmer-Labor Party. He assured his Council Bluffs listeners that there was no real difference between Democrats and Republicans and insisted that "Bread and meat, not liquor" was the real issue of the upcoming election between Hoover and Roosevelt.

By mid-August both the Nonpareil and Omaha Bee-News were duly reporting the murder of suspected Kansas City racketeer Angelo Savigliano, alias Angelo Morrow, who was then living in Council Bluffs at 806 Avenue H. Savigliano was taken for a "gangland ride and shot through the back 10 times" and dumped on the highway north of Glenwood. There was also news reports of the Farmer's Holiday Association "milk war" up around Sioux City where 1,500 farmers had blocked the highways to force dairy companies into paying them a higher price. Then on the 21st the newspapers announced a meeting at Dunlap of farmers from Carroll, Crawford, Monona, Pottawattamie, and Harrison counties planning to blockade the roads into Omaha using "moral persuasion". The Bee-News reported that spokesman Clinton Savery called the Holiday a "prosperity restorer" and volunteers could go to the tourist camp in Missouri Valley to be assigned to 12 hour shifts.

"Strikers' Picket Highway" announced the Nonpareil headline on Monday August 22nd as pickets began to appear on the major paved roads leading into Council Bluffs. That included US Highways 30S and 75 which entered town from the north along the old Lincoln Highway. Some five miles east of Council Bluffs a group of 40 men from Harrison County had blocked US Highway 6. Sheriff Lainson was in Des Moines and Deputy Frank Owen sent several deputies to the Woodland School north of Council Bluffs on US Highway 30 where pickets gathered in the parking lot.

Sheriff Lainson hurried back from the state capitol and quickly recruited six additional deputies. On August 23rd the Sheriff announced on promises of no violence and free milk distribution on North Main supervised by the Council Bluffs Central Labor Union. The Sheriff was "allowing peaceful picketing but no rough stuff." The Nonpareil reported that traffic through the Farmer's Livestock Marketing Association at North 10th Street and Avenue G had "fallen off considerably" and similar pickets had appeared at Onawa, Spencer, Hawarden, the Missouri River bridge to Plattsmouth, and on the US 30 bridge to Blair.

The last major route blocked into Council Bluffs was US Route 34 which then entered Council Bluffs from the south along present day Harry Langdon Boulevard. A mass of men with a banner declaring "We Want Better Prices" appeared on the highway from Mosquito Creek south to the intersection with the unpaved Shortline Highway between Treynor and South Omaha. There were also reports of a meeting at Red Oak led by Lee Humphreys to block Highway 34 down there as well. And it was along Highway 34 where the worst "rough stuff" took place. The trouble began after picketers ignored Deputy Owens request to quit standing in the highway and only grew worse after a heated exchange arose after the pickets stopped B.H. Brandt's cream truck. Deputy Owens warned them that they were "breaking into jail" if they halted trucks by force.

The pickets on US 34 paid Owens little mind and the highway was blocked with telephone poles near the Iowa School for the Deaf. Truckdrivers were stopped and warned to turn-around and not to take their produce into Council Bluffs or Omaha. More than words greeted the few truckers that attempted to run the blockade. In response, Sheriff Lainson hired 98 special deputies at $3.50 a day and swore that he was "going to fight it out if it takes 5,000 deputies and $50,000". The Special Deputies, identified by yellow bands around their left arms, were divided into three patrols overseen by Deputies Kinsell, Williams, and Lammert and escorts were offered through the blockades to any truck driver who requested one. Sheriff Lainson blamed the disturbance on outside agitators, mostly "from Sioux City, the toughest town in Iowa, and are not farmers at all." The Sheriff warned that, "If the Pottawattamie County Jail bulges with pickets it will just have to bulge".

The mass of Pottawattamie deputies mostly made their way to the south edge of Council Bluffs where the largest pickets were set up near the Iowa School for the Deaf. According to the newspaper, 1,000 people blocked the road at the present intersection of Harry Langdon Boulevard, Wabash Avenue, and Iowa Highway 92 although actual picketers might have been outnumbered by folks just out gawking. At first, nothing much amounted from the milling, shoving, threats, and curses that resulted. The Sheriff's office also took the time to cite truck driver Lynn Alderman for "speeding and reckless driving" after he was permitted through the pickets on Highway 34.

And then Sheriff Lainson tried another tactic to open the road and on Wednesday night he sent an automobile loaded with tear-gas straight through the pickets. According to one report, a female reporter from Council Bluffs got the worst dose of it as the choking mob "replied with a barrage of sticks, stones, pop bottles, and other missiles", including a railroad

Some of the graffiti left behind by 84 years of bored prisoners.

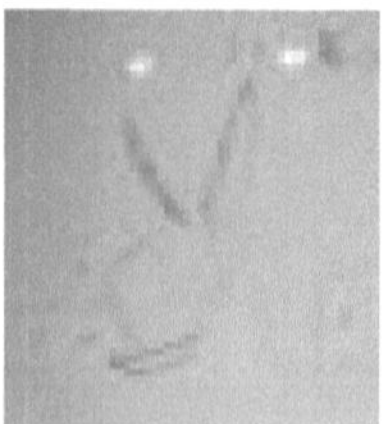

tie, and threw the tear gas into Mosquito Creek. The windows of the tear-gas car were smashed and Special Deputy (and Major in the Iowa National Guard) Henry Hall and Council Bluffs Policemen Al Watson and Phil Mozier were all injured by both flying glass and their own gas.

During the resulting violence many picketers were arrested for "unlawful assembly" and hauled down to the Squirrel Cage although reliable numbers remain debatable. The Nonpareil dutifully noted that those arrested came from Crescent, Missouri Valley, Mapleton, Onawa, and Logan. Another batch of 13 picketers, mostly from Denison, had been arrested earlier near McPherson and Bennett Streets where US 6 entered town. A.J. Schweery of Panama, Iowa was arrested near Johnson Hill about seven miles east of Council Bluffs after he blocked US 6 with his truck. Harry Rink of Neola was arrested trying to intercept trucks headed down West Broadway for the Douglas Street Bridge to Omaha. With the Squirrel Cage packed to potentially its fullest extent ever, all prisoners were served bean soup for supper that night.

The worst of Wednesday's night violence was along the stretch of US 34 between tracks of the Milwaukee Railroad and the Iowa School for the Deaf but the highway was blocked again by Thursday morning. In addition to the hundreds of people standing and sitting in the road, picketers had blocked the highway with a 20 foot telephone pole, a pile of brush, three plank barriers, and a six inch piece of iron with spikes. Bee-News columnist T.W. McCullough warned the "hard-boiled Sheriff of Pottawattamie County" that "Tear bombs and hair-trigger deputies could well be dispensed with in his dealing with the farmer pickets. . . There are other ways of killing a cat than by kissing it to death."

Indeed, the tear-gas and mass arrest brought growing national attention with syndicated Hearst newspaper columnist "Bugs" Baer commenting from the campaign trail on the "Ioway" farmers who had "won the first battle of Pottawattamie…" Generally sympathetic to the Holiday strikers, according to Baer "The biggest worry is how to get them back on the farm after they've seen Council Bluffs." At the same time, the Council Bluffs Central Labor Union met a few blocks from the jail at the Railroad YMCA on 1st Avenue to declare their "full sympathy and support" to the Holiday picketers. The Labor-News reported the resignation of four unionized deputies and quoted Sheriff Lainson as saying that it was "a dirty shame they won't let an unemployed man work who has the chance to make a few dollars."

Many others, veterans of the highway milk wars around Sioux City and Le Mars, were even more incensed and on August 25th the Nonpareil reported that a "1,000 men" from Woodbury County and elsewhere in northwest Iowa were headed to the Squirrel Cage to bust the picketers out. The Iowa National Guard announced intentions to move the 168th Infantry in from Des Moines if needed and Time magazine quoted one of those headed to Council Bluffs as demanding the release of all prisoners "by nightfall or else - I'm prepared to meet my God tonight as well as any other time."

On Thursday morning the prisoners were served a breakfast of oatmeal with milk, a bun, and black coffee while Sheriff Lainson distributed seven machine and sub-machine guns and several riot guns to his deputies at the Squirrel Cage. The Sheriff's Special Deputies were armed with new pick handles and baseball bats and were used to "move on" the thousands of spectators and sympathizers, "most of them curious Council Bluffs residents" who had congregated at the Courthouse and Jail. But the crowd only grew after news of an accidental shooting inside the Squirrel Cage swept across town. While demonstrating a riot gun, Deputy Kinsell inadvertently shot and killed Special Deputy Claude Dale and severely injured Joe Ludwig in front of Jailer Elmer Lainson, his wife Louise, and their two daughters. Special Deputy Dale was a 36 year old bus driver who lived at 405 Damon Street.

The "Squirrel Cage" was filled to the brim with prisoners and a crowd gathered. Fearing a riot, Sheriff Lainson distributed seven machine and sub-machine guns and several riot guns to his deputies.

The first batch of "embittered farmers" from northwest Iowa arrived in Council Bluffs late Thursday afternoon to the growing hubbub downtown. F. Raymond Snyder of Kingsley, Iowa presented Sheriff Lainson with their ultimatum and the Sheriff attended a "peace conference" held up the street at the Hotel Chieftain with Council Bluffs Mayor Myrtue and the leaders of the pickets. At the same time, the imprisoned picketers in the Squirrel Cage were fed dinner: a boiled potato with gravy, a small piece of meat, and a slice of bread.

Cool heads ultimately prevailed before the situation escalated totally out of control and the picketers were freed from the Squirrel Cage not long after dinner. Judge DeWitt had already freed four of those arrested because they were minors and nine cases had been dismissed due to lack of evidence. The last 61 picketers were out of jail by 6 PM Thursday evening, 16 of them had been found guilty and were free on $200 bonds and the rest were free on $100 bonds and promises to appear back in court in September. Most of the bond money had been put up by a handful of local farmers.

Chieftain Hotel, two blocks from the Squirrel Cage jail, where Sheriff Lainson and Mayor Myrtue met in a "peace conference" with embittered farmers in an effort to forestall a march on the jail.

The freed picketers received a rousing welcome back on the blocked highways where John Uhl told of their mistreatment and the "intolerable conditions" at the jail. The jailed farmers, who were mostly from western Iowa, remained indignant of the accommodations provided by Pottawattamie County and complained that the Squirrel Cage lacked cots, mattresses, or chairs and that they "had to stand up or take turns squatting along the wall" the entire time.

Emboldened by success, one picketer assured the Bee-News that "We won't start anything, but we're more than willing to finish anything the deputies start...The deputies started that rumpus Wednesday night with tear gas, and I guess they didn't finish it." The Sheriff's office estimated 3,000 Holiday strikers across Pottawattamie County with 1,500 of them manning the pickets on US 34. Bales of hay had also been set across Iowa Highway 7, which entered Council Bluffs on Canning Street, and Iowa Highway 24.

The Bee-News noted that Sheriff's patrols remained a quarter-mile or more from the pickets on US 34 which remained a flashpoint of hostility where any stranger was accused of being a spy until they could prove themselves otherwise. Eight stores in Council Bluffs provided food for the barricades on US 34 and a Mrs. Spencer who lived near the Iowa School for the Deaf served them coffee. Reverend J.R. McNichols, pastor at Epworth Methodist in Council Bluffs, arrived with lunch meat to distribute and told the newspaper that he hoped the pickets brought more attention to the problems faced by Iowa farmers.

The jailed farmers were indignant of the poor accommodations at the "Squirrel Cage" jail.

Sheriff Lainson increased the number of Special Deputies to 150 and called on southwest Iowa farmers to be "patient a little longer." And there was news that the Farmer's Holiday continued to spread with reports of pickets at Shenandoah, the bridge across the Missouri to Nebraska City, and the highway between Blair and Omaha.

Rain turned the unpaved Shortline Highway between Treynor and South Omaha into mud and only seemed to encourage the mosquitoes that swarmed the picketers at night. Most of them found refuge in Ben Sieck's barn, their "principal billet" located across the highway from the Iowa School for the Deaf. All vehicles were subject to be stopped and searched although at least one farmer managed to speed through the blockade with a calf sitting in the rumble seat of his coupe.

On Saturday Ed Perrien, the manager of Pinecrest Farms, was forced to leave eight cans of milk with the pickets out on Highway 6 east of Council Bluffs. At the request of Bernard Beno, who owned Pinecrest, Deputy Kinsell took 20 deputies out to the picket line to rescue the milk and bring it into Council Bluffs. Before long, the Holiday pickets had dumped 800 gallons of milk on the side of the road and national press coverage only intensified. One agitator announced, "Action is action. To hell with the Department of Agriculture, to hell with Hoover and to hell with you newspapermen!" There were also rumors in the Bee-News that some sort of agreement was in the works between the Holiday Association and the big dairies in Omaha and Council Bluffs. On Saturday night the mosquitoes were kept down by the huge bonfires that warmed the pickets manning the blockades across US 30S-75, 6, 34, and Iowa 7 into Council Bluffs, the US 30 bridge to Blair, and the bridge to Plattsmouth.

The manager of Pinecrest Farms was forced by the pickets to leave eight cans of milk on U.S. Highway 6 east of Council Bluffs. Twenty deputies rescued the milk and brought it to Council Bluffs.

On Sunday morning the 28th Omahan M.H. Cruise received a lacerated eyeball at the pickets on US 34. Cruise was a passenger in a truck driven by Harold Walner of Tabor and someone threw a club through the front window. Walner was also slightly injured by glass but the pickets allowed them through after they discovered the truck was empty. There were only about 50 picketers out on the highways into Council Bluffs on Sunday while Omaha Mayor Metcalfe was working on a solution with the dairy companies.

On Monday August 29th Council Bluffs remained "under complete blockade". According to the Bee-News only eleven trucks from Iowa had made it to the Omaha livestock market. G.W. Goodland, manager of the Farmers Livestock Marketing in Council Bluffs, reported that no hogs had come in for the past four days at a time of the year when they usually saw 250-350 hogs daily. Plans were also announced for a Midwestern governor's conference in Sioux City to deal with the Holiday Association. Nebraska Governor Bryan blamed "agitators from Iowa" for crossing the Missouri to cause trouble and suggested that the farmers "should picket the Republican party" instead.

Out on the highways, the Bee-News reported the "Iowa fair price picketers" remained in high spirits. At night especially the blockades were enlivened with the song: "We're on the highway now/We're not behind the plow/We'll win at last/They'll never get past/For we're on the highway now!" By Tuesday August 30th the pickets had started to blockade the roads into Omaha from the west while the Douglas County Sheriff vowed to keep the highways open. At that time the Omaha city limits ended at 72nd Street and Holiday pickets appeared at 84th and Military Avenue, 90th and Maple, 92nd and Dodge, 90th and Pacific, and at 95th and Center.

And then the Holiday Strike of 1932 was called off on a Wednesday night, a week after the tear-gas attack on US 34. A "truce" was announced by Holiday Association leaders Milo Reno and John Chalmers after 14 pickets were shot at outside of Cherokee, Iowa. The Holiday strikers around Council Bluffs were less than enthusiastic at the news of peace and had planned to move on to Shenandoah where produce was being taken and shipped to Omaha via railroad.

Sheriff Lainson announced that all roads into Council Bluffs were open by Friday morning and dismissed all but a half-dozen Special Deputies. The pickets vanished west of Omaha as well as the Farmer's Holiday came to an abrupt end. The Bee-News reported that the retail price of a quart of milk in Omaha and Council Bluffs would soon increase from 8 to 9 cents as part of the agreement by dairies to pay farmers $1.80 per 100 pounds of base milk, an increase of 50 cents.

Sheriff Lainson was not the Republican candidate for Sheriff that November 1932 when the newspaper reported a rare occurrence at the jail. Just a few days before the election the Nonpareil reported on renovations at the Squirrel Cage when for the first and only time in the jail's history the jailer supervised prisoners as they excavated a north-south tunnel underneath the cell-block. The tunnel, which was blocked in the 1970's, was meant to provide outside air "more readily heated and far more comfortable" than the "old stale air system with an outlet but no inlet below". The newspaper quoted Jailer Pat Lainson as saying that it was "bad enough for a man to bc shut in a jail without the ordinary elements of sanitation being ignored. Mrs. Lainson, myself and our family live in the building. We try to make the place as decent and respectable as we would have our own home". Jailer Lainson also assured the newspaper that the Squirrel Cage was "one of the cleanest, most sanitary, and best kept jails in the state."

Nonetheless, the Republican candidate Gillaspy was defeated by Democrat Joe Perry by almost 4,500 votes. Perry and his wife Eunice lived at 913 1st Avenue in Council Bluffs and he would take over as the new Sheriff of Pottawattamie County, complete with all privileges and headaches, including the continued upkeep of the 47 year old Squirrel Cage. Percy Lainson was later appointed Warden of Iowa's Ft. Madison penitentiary where he was reputedly "tough but fair" and in 1952 the one-time overseer of the Squirrel Cage

The entire fourth floor of the Squirrel Cage was intended as a spacious apartment for the jailer and his family. Smells from the primitive sewer system of the three story cage below sometimes made for less than ideal conditions.

said that "In the long run, the protection of society will be best achieved through constructive treatment of offenders from conviction on, including adequate preparation for release and helpful supervision thereafter." Lainson was named Warden of the Year by the National Warden's Association in 1955 and eventually retired to Council Bluffs where he died in 1964. One of the Historical Society's few mementos from Lainson's tenure as Sheriff of Pottawattamie County is the 1928 wanted poster for drug addict Marvin Mercer.

Sheriff Joe Perry and his successors would be dogged over the next decade with innuendoes of cash-stuffed envelopes as a variety of illegal casinos ran full tilt around the county. This included the infamous Chez Paree in Carter Lake and the Riviera and Stork Club just south of Council Bluffs which also attracted the interests of Kansas City racketeer Charles Binaggio. At the same time, the notorious Meyer Lansky operated the Kennel Club Greyhound Track in league with the Council Bluffs Park Department.

The notorious Meyer Lansky operated the Kennel Club Greyhound Track in league with the Council Bluffs Park Department.

And for some the hard times continued. In 1939, in the month between June 27 to July 26, 23 people were housed at the Squirrel Cage for intoxication, three for disturbing the peace, four for being drunk while disturbing the peace, two for illegal train riding, nine for vagrancy, two for begging in the street, one for desertion of wife and child, and one unlucky soul who found himself spending time charged with begging and vagrancy both.

Recent Prisoners

What was probably a spur-of-the-moment decision in early May 1942 ultimately cost Omaha tailor Joe Letak his life. Harry McAtee, proprietor of the Inn Tavern at 527 West Broadway, reported that someone had stolen his money pouch containing $23.95 from behind the bar. Council Bluffs Detectives McDaniel and Tisher soon booked Joe Letak on suspicion of the crime. Letak was arrested at the nearby Empire Buffet after McAtee's missing money pouch was found empty in the bathroom. Unable to come up with the $500 bond to get released, he was hauled down Squirrel Cage. After 19 days sitting in jail, Letak apparently decided to take a nap on the third-floor catwalk that once encircled the Cage. He apparently fell almost 20 feet onto the cement floor below and died soon after at Mercy Hospital with a fractured skull.

Sometimes a small town girl in trouble in the big city is sadly not always just another Hollywood cliché. In July 1945, 22 year old Charlean Rutledge from Clarion, Iowa attempted suicide at the Squirrel Cage by breaking a glass against the bars of her cell and slitting her wrists. She'd been arrested for writing a bad check and was being held awaiting action by the Grand Jury. Ms. Rutledge had only been in Council Bluffs about three weeks, was living at 537 5th Avenue, and was working as a waitress.

In August 1947 Judge Charles Roe gave Robert Miller a six month stay in the Squirrel Cage after his "rampage with a loaded revolver". Miller had been arrested for taking a shot at his ex-wife who walking down North 14th Street with Fred Foote. Miller then forced Foote into a taxi-cab where he threatened Foote's life and, at gunpoint, forced the cabbie to elude the police. He then threatened Patrolmen C.J. Turpen and L.G. Slusher with his gun before officers wrestled him to the ground. Oddly enough, Miller's court-appointed attorney was the Judge's son, Charles M. Roe.

In January 1949 Otto Gudath and his wife were appointed Jailer and Matron. Gudath was born in Louisville, Kentucky and had moved to Council Bluffs in 1912. For 36 years of his life Gudath had worked as a butcher, including a stint at A.W. Huber's grocery at 122 West Broadway. Otto and his wife's first year at the Squirrel Cage would prove an interesting one.

Early that July 1949, Basil Foote Jr. of 1703 Avenue J wound up in the Squirrel Cage after violently protecting the honor of his wife at the Diamond Tavern at 16th Street and West Broadway. Foote was drinking at the Diamond with noted hoodlum Earl Limerick, who was then living at 1126 5th Avenue, when Limerick reputedly made disparaging comments about Mrs. Foote. Basil left, walked over to the nearby home of his mother-in-law at 1627 Avenue D, headed back to the bar with a five inch ice pick, and proceeded to buy Limerick a drink. As Limerick raised his glass, Foote pulled out the ice pick, declared "This is what I think of you", and stabbed him in the chest. Foote fled the Diamond as Limerick pulled the pick out and began chasing his assailment up North 16th Street with the ice pick in one hand. Bleeding heavily, Limerick only lasted a few blocks before he collapsed in a parking lot. Foote was soon captured and, according to the newspaper, boasted during booking "Sure, I killed Earl Limerick. I hope he dies. Gimme a piece of paper and I will write out a statement admitting it." Limerick, however, survived the attack and was soon conscious enough to describe how the ice pick was "up to the handle when I pulled it out." Earl's brother Tom had an equally deserved reputation and led a gang with Maurice Denning that "looted a score of banks in the midwest" during the mid-1930's. Tom Limerick was eventually captured and shipped to Alcatraz where he was killed attempting to escape in May 1938.

End of the Rotary

The 1958 election of Democrat Emmett Hannan as Sheriff would force the department into the modern era. At the time of Hannan's election the Sheriff's office, which oversaw Iowa's second largest county and 6th largest city, was still housed in a few rooms on the first floor of the 1888 Courthouse adjacent to the jail with similar, smaller operations out in Avoca. Hannan made several changes in the department and named Roy Wichael as his new Chief Deputy. Wichael had worked for years with his father as switchmen for the Milwaukee Railroad in Council Bluffs. Sheriff Hannan also replaced the staff at the Squirrel Cage with Mr. and Mrs. McDaniel taking the place of Otto Gudath and his wife as Jailer and Matron. Tim Ryan of 3037 Avenue A replaced Arthur Schuelzky as Night Jailer and W.E. Glaser was named Relief Jailer. A month after the election in December 1958 Council Bluffs resident John Barrett escaped out of the Squirrel Cage while being held on robbery charges. He was soon re-captured and sentenced to 11 years in Anamosa.

Electric lights were finally added to the cells in 1960 ending 75 years of darkness.

In 1960 Sheriff Hannan had a heart attack in office and died. He was replaced that May by his Chief Deputy, Roy Wichael. Sheriff Wichael quickly took even more steps to modernize the department, including moving the office into seven rooms in the basement of the Courthouse. That same year Wilman T. "Bill" Foster and his wife Louise were hired as Jailer and Matron of the Squirrel Cage. Bill Foster had come to Council Bluffs from Naper, Nebraska back in 1932.

The county jail would prove a continuous contention for Sheriff Wichael and in November 1960 the Squirrel Cage was closed for renovations. District Court Judges had not sentenced anyone to the Squirrel Cage since mid-September as the facility was "unfit because of health and safety reasons." Five prisoners were escorted across the street to the Council Bluffs City Jail on the second floor of City Hall and three others were taken down to the Page County Jail at Clarinda. According to Jailer Bill Foster, "It's going to be pretty quiet around here until we are back in business again." Sheriff Roy Wichael held an "open house" for the public at the county detention facilities in both Council Bluffs and Avoca. The costs of renovation and improvements were estimated at $4,000 and included electric lights in individual cells for the first time and communal toilets. When the Squirrel Cage re-opened, America's largest rotary jail had been fixed in place and has not rotated since.

The crank once used to rotate the three story 90,000 pound drum was no longer needed after the cage was locked into place in 1960.

Nonetheless, the last nine years would prove to be some of the Squirrel Cage's most interesting and contentious as its continued use became a source of head-shaking amazement and escapes became all the more common. In spite of various improvements, the county jail remained

Two prisoners escaped in 1960 by prying open a metal plate in the floor of a cell (left) and climbing through a 15 foot tunnel that led to a cellar door (right). The lock they smashed to open the cellar door (above) is on display in the jail museum.

a sore spot with Sheriff Wichael who complained to the Des Moines Register in 1961 that the Squirrel Cage had been "condemned a dozen times by the county board."

John Dominguez wound up in the Squirrel Cage on Halloween night 1961, charged with reckless driving. Dominguez became a trustee at the jail but after finishing washing dishes on November 12 he walked out the door and into the night. He stole a car in Council Bluffs and headed west but wound up getting arrested out in Englewood, Colorado. Sentenced to two years probation, Dominguez returned to Council Bluffs and was attempting to get a duplicate drivers license at the Pottawattamie County Courthouse next door to the jail when he was recognized by a deputy. He was quoted in the Nonpareil claming that, "I didn't know it was an escape. I thought it was a breach of promise." He pled guilty and was sentenced to a year in Anamosa and fined $25.

Two prisoners escaped out of the Jail sometime on a Sunday night in June 1962 and no one even noticed until the Monday afternoon. John Barrett, who had escaped from the Squirrel Cage in 1958, was back in jail for violating parole. He had been let out of Anamosa but found himself in trouble back home in Council Bluffs after he got into a fight with three juveniles who claimed that he'd stolen their wallets. Barrett was joined in the break-out by Roy Owens who was being held for breaking and entering. Owens had been arrested at Viaduct Lanes at 105 North 12th Street on May 1 after a shoot-out with police officers Ed Dinovo and William Pettit who used tear gas to flush him out of the bowling alley. Sheriff Wichael considered Owens "extremely dangerous". The pair had pried open a metal plate in the floor of a cell near the toilets and then made their way down into the 15 foot long tunnel under the Squirrel Cage that led to a cellar door on the north side of the jail. They smashed the lock on the gate and fled over the spiked iron fence into the night. The lock smashed by Owens and Barrett during their escape is on permanent display at the Jail.

Two months later on a Wednesday night in August 1962 a "miniature riot" broke out in the jail's bullpen after prisoners tore out electric conduits, broke all the lights, and plugged three floor drains, flooding the first floor until water "ran out the front door…" The inmates "made a racket that could be heard on Broadway" and beat fellow prisoner Lowell Carter for not joining in. The rumpus finally came to an end after deputies threatened to use tear-gas on them. A dozen prisoners were put on bread and water until Sheriff Wichael was "sure they have learned their lesson", their bedding was taken away, and they were not allowed magazines, cards, radios, or any other entertainment. Forced to clean up the mess, "None of the prisoners could offer any reason for their actions..." Phil Jones, thought to be one of instigators, was taken across the street to the City Jail and soon sent along to Anamosa to serve a seven year sentence. Thursday night, however, brought another racket, just not quite as loud. Six prisoners remained on bread and water and Earl Vaughn and Ken Bingle were taken over to City Jail. "They have no beef," proclaimed Sheriff Wichael, and would "stay on bread and water until they quiet down nights." All prisoners were finally served a full meal for lunch on Saturday consisting of three eggs, fried potatoes, a vegetable, bread, and coffee.

The most frequent resident of the Squirrel Cage through the years was Richard Wilson, better known as "The Pennsylvania Kid." (Photo courtesy Nancy Parish.)

Perhaps the most frequent resident of the Squirrel Cage through the years was Richard Wilson, better known by his hobo moniker "The Pennsylvania Kid". Wilson left Franklin, Pennsylvania behind and spent most of his life riding the rails across the country which naturally led to many stops in Council Bluffs. In fact, between 1931 and 1967 he was fingerprinted 92 times in Pottawattamie County, typically charged with vagrancy or illegal train riding. Wilson, who claimed to be "America's dirtiest hobo", was first elected King of the Hobos in 1963 at the Hobo Convention held annually at Britt, Iowa since 1900. Wilson was re-elected in 1966 and wound up back at the Squirrel Cage for two weeks after a fistfight the next year. During his stay at the jail Wilson was escorted up to the Council Bluffs Savings Bank by Deputy Sheriff Earl Pace to pay the fee on his safety deposit box. Deputy Pace told the newspaper that Wilson "smelled clean" in spite of his self-promotion and called him "a bum who

Johnson Pharmacy as it appeared when John Croghan broke into it in 1964.

isn't a bum" and "the kind of guy you get to like." In 1968 the Pennsylvania Kid beat out Slow Motion Shorty to reclaim his title at Britt and won his last election as Hobo King in 1971. The Pennsylvania Kid eventually caught the "Westbound" and is buried at the Hobo's Memorial Section of the Britt cemetery.

Michigan resident Wayne Simonsen and Leroy Gilmore escaped out of the Squirrel Cage in October 1963. Simonsen was in jail for grand larceny after breaking into pay telephones and taking the money and Gilmore was in jail for a parole violation. Their escape was discovered by a state parole officer who showed up to take Gilmore back to Anamosa. Gilmore had been sentenced in 1959 to 10 years in prison but had been paroled that spring. It was suspected that outside help once again shoved saw blades through the wire mesh that covered the jail's windows.

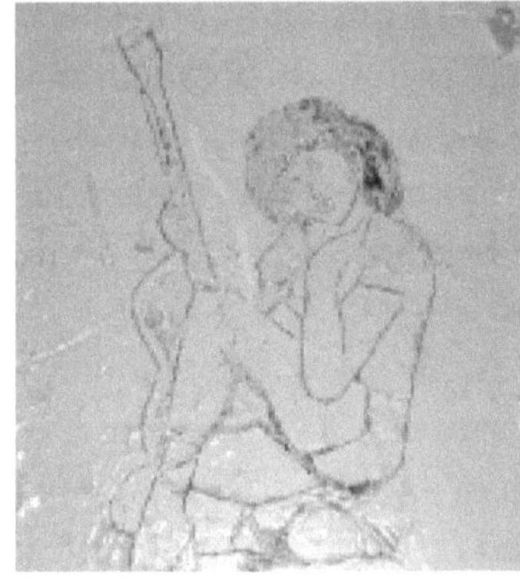

Grafitti from juvenile section of the jail.

Another violent escape occurred during October 1964 when John Croghan of Crescent fought his way out of the jail. Croghan had been arrested earlier that year for breaking into the Johnson Pharmacy but fled the state while free on bond. A bail bondsman brought Croghan back to Council Bluffs from Denver and he was awaiting trial for breaking and entering. Jailer Bill Foster was returning a prisoner to the third floor cells but "When I unlocked the door Croghan dashed out...I hit him on the back of the head with the door padlock I had. It seemed to slow him down a bit." Nonetheless, Foster and Croghan fought down the three flights of metal stairs with the prisoner losing his shoes in the process. Croghan managed to flee out the front door and ran down the alley in his socks only to be re-captured a few days later.

That same year a $440,000 bond issue to construct a new county jail failed at the polls and the District Court ordered the Squirrel Cage closed for six months due to its various "inadequacies and deplorable conditions." One indication of the Squirrel Cage's future came in October 1965 when a visiting official of the U.S. Department of the Interior recommended that the structure should be preserved as an "oddity." Nonetheless, the Squirrel Cage's time as a jail were truly numbered.

Jail Matron Louise Foster died in 1966 and her husband Bill retired from the Sheriff's Department two years later. Bill Foster, the last Jailer to rotate the Squirrel Cage, lived at 1510 Avenue A until his death in 1979. The Fosters place as Jailer and Matron of the county jail was taken over by Jesse Poor and his wife Gladys.

In October 1966 prisoners Milo Constandine and Roger Steele escaped out of the Squirrel Cage after using an 18" bar to saw a half-inch steel lock that secured the fire door on the south side of the jail. The duo then fled down the fire escape and over the spiked iron fence. Steele was awaiting sentencing after pleading guilty to burglarizing a store in Avoca and Constandine had been arrested trying to break into a Council Bluffs tavern. One prisoner refused to join them and stayed behind.

The "Squirrel Cage" in its final days as a county jail. (Photo courtesy Dr. Robert Warner.)

According to the Nonpareil in December 1968, the Iowa Department of Social Services informed the Pottawattamie County Board that the jail should "not be used to confine inmates" and cited a laundry list of reasons compiled by William Swassing, Iowa's Chief Jail Inspector and former Council Bluffs Chief of Police. According to Swassing's report, deficiencies at the county jail included lack of individual cells with all prisoners housed together regardless of the severity of their crimes. Swassing pointed out that the jail was unsafe for officers due to numerous blind spots and noted that the "jailer refuses to enter the cell block alone." Staff also had limited control over the cell block while the 83 year old building's electrical wiring was "old, inadequate, and exposed," the lighting poor, and the plumbing "old, deteriorated, and often backs up" making sanitation "extremely difficult." Furthermore, the kitchen was too small, the roof leaked with pans placed everywhere whenever it rained, the food supplies froze solid on occasion in winter, and there was no place for "recreation, rehabilitation, segregated quarters for work release inmates or counseling and visitation...."

Ambitious prisoners dug a hole through a rusted iron wall to make one of the jail's last escapes. The four even left a note behind: "Dear Sir: I sincerely hope that this escape will help you get a new jail because you need one."

While Pottawattamie County officials attempted to find a way to keep the jail operational, one of the last escapes out of the Squirrel Cage took place in January 1969 after a group of ambitious prisoners managed to pry a steel leg off a metal table attached to one of the walls. They spent the next five nights digging a hole through the rusted iron wall in the bullpen and then through three layers of brick. To muffle the noise of their excavation, the prisoners disconnected a nearby steam radiator so that it would bang all night long and used wet newspapers to cover their work during the day. Finally, on a Wednesday night, four men fled out the hole leaving seven prisoners who declined to join them in their bid for freedom. The four even left a note behind: "Dear Sir: I sincerely hope that this escape will help you get a new jail because you need one." The escapees included Fred Pond who was in jail for stealing a car and parole violations; Mike Rhoades was in jail for larceny; Ralph Taylor of Kansas City, Kansas was incarcerated for grand larceny; and Bill Jorgensen was serving time for breaking and entering and robbery. The four fled to Rhoades' father's home on North 15th Street to try and get a ride to Omaha. Rhoades' father refused and told him he was taking him back to jail but the four apparently forced him to drive them across the river. The senior Rhoades then called police and reported the escape and three of the four were back in custody within a few hours. As for the note, Sheriff Wichael commented that "I didn't know they cared that much..."

In spite of the County Board's pleas to officials in Des Moines to bring the jail up to code, the Squirrel Cage was closed for good on December 1, 1969 following the failure of a $220,000 bond issue to build a new correctional facility. The eleven prisoners held inside were sent to the Page County Jail in Clarinda at a cost of $10 each per day with an additional $10 charge for each female prisoner. The Squirrel Cage's last Jailer and Matron, Jesse

Mystery author Elizabeth Dean lead the charge on the part of the Historcal Society to save the "Squirrel Cage."

and Gladys Poor, were prepared to move out by the middle of the month. At the same time, Frederic Schlott, Chairman of the Council Bluffs Park Board, was leading efforts to preserve the jail as a good bet for a tourist draw. Demolition was narrowly avoided in part due to Liz Dean and Gwen Woodward from the Historical Society. The Council Bluffs Park Board purchased the Jail for $5,000 the next year and agreed to operate the property with the Historical Society of Pottawattamie County.

Although over $10,000 was spent on badly needed renovations, the Squirrel Cage was once again threatened with demolition in the late 1970's by Pottawattamie County officials seeking to enlarge the parking lot of the new courthouse. The Des Moines Register profiled the battle in a June 1977 article on whether or not the Jail was a "mechanical marvel of historic importance" or "an affront to taxpayers who

The Historical Society has extensively renovated the "Squirrel Cage" jail to avoid its deterioration from weathering and age.

are being cuffed for nearly $5 million for a new courthouse". The Pottawattamie County Board of Supervisors unanimously voted that the Jail should be "fixed up, destroyed, or moved" with Supervisor Don Smith declaring the 1885 building "an eyesore..." A reprieve was announced that same month when the Council Bluffs City Council voted to lease the Squirrel Cage to the Historical Society of Pottawattamie County for a dollar a year. The next year, the Jail was sold to the Historical Society for $8001. The Historical Society of Pottawattamie County has continued to operate the Squirrel Cage ever since as one of the most unique museums in the country.

Epilogue

These are just a handful of the many tales that took place at the Squirrel Cage Jail in Council Bluffs and we hope you have enjoyed them. If you know any more, or are willing to contribute in any way to the jail's ongoing maintenance and continued efforts to preserve our shared history, please contact the Historical Society of Pottawattamie County at (712) 323-2509 or through the society's website: www.thehistoricalsociety.org.

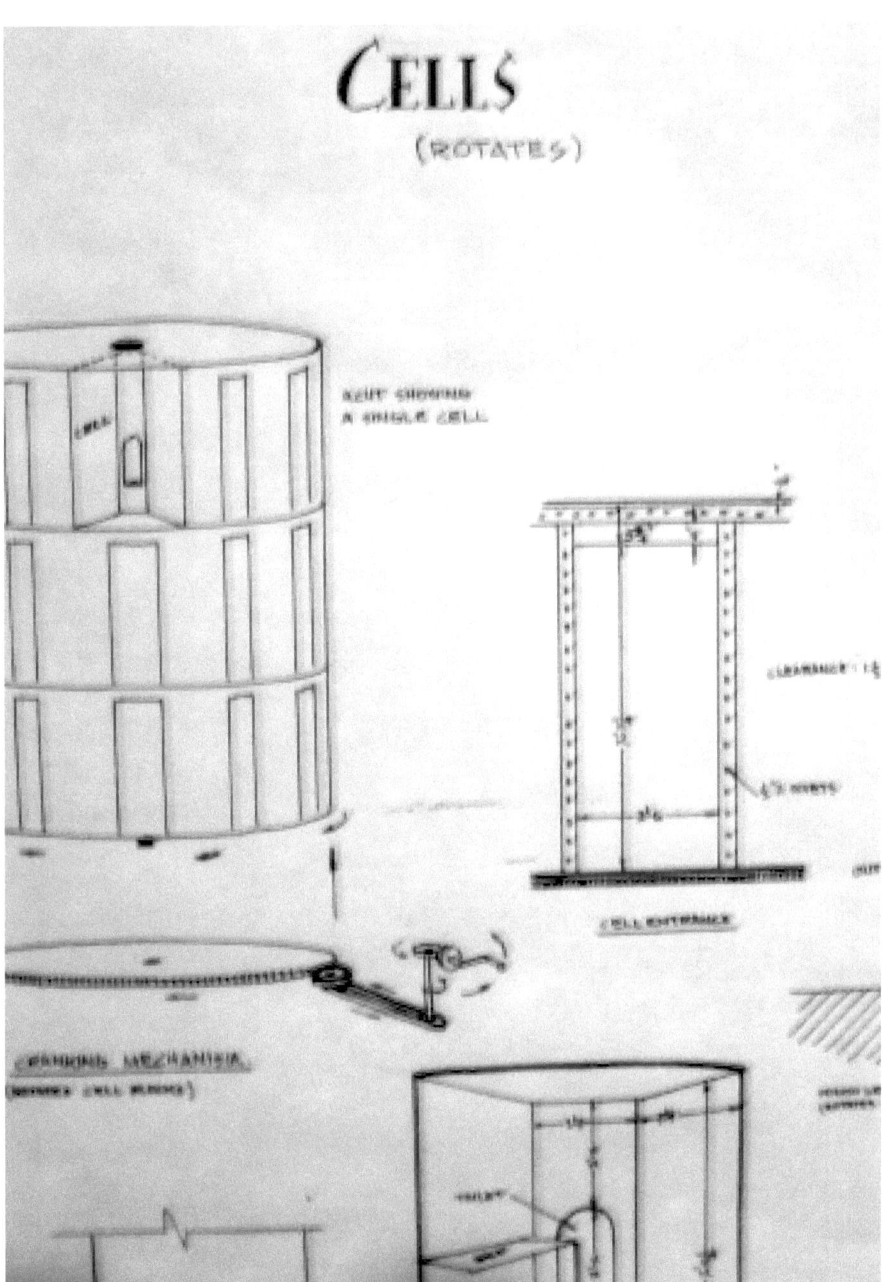
CELLS
(ROTATES)

www.ingramcontent.com/pod-product-compliance
Ingram Content Group UK Ltd.
Pitfield, Milton Keynes, MK11 3LW, UK
UKHW041837200726
13854UKWH00003BA/1186